A FOG OF GREY VOICES

**A Poem by
Hugh Oliver**

For my brother John

Copyright © 2011 Hugh P. Oliver

All rights reserved. Except for brief excerpts used as part of a review, no part of this publication may be reproduced, stored in a retrieval system, or transmitted, in any form or by any means, photocopying, electronic, mechanical, recording, or otherwise, without prior written permission of the copyright holder.

Hugh Oliver
123 Scadding Avenue - #863
Toronto, ON
M5A 4J3

ISBN 978-1-105-35671-1

To see life clearly and to see it whole.
(Matthew Arnold's Uncertainty Principle)

Sat at my desk of polished rosewood grain,
I poise my pen above the empty page,
Seeking the imagery for what I want to say,
Searching among the memories of old age.

Panorama of night,
Of cosmic serenity
With shimmering stars
In fanciful configurations;
A universe
Cathedraled in light
Expanding and contracting
Through space/time,
Back to the beginning,
Forward to the end --
If there was a beginning,
If there will be an end;
If there will be a beginning,
If there was an end.
A universe
In which the speed of light is absolute
And space bends.

In the beginning, God (or so it went)
Created in six days the Firmament
Till Physics with a Bang (or so it goes)
Achieved about the same result -- who knows?

In fifteen billion years -- well give or take
A year or two. It's difficult to make
A universe from bits that whirl away.
Like Rome, it doesn't happen in a day.

At my conception,
At my beginning,
Hardly immaculate,
On the contrary, a routine encounter
Catalysed by a bottle of sherry
And, like most conceptions,
Lacking intent…

At my conception,
At my beginning,
My universe was void and without form
And darkness was upon the face of the waters.

At my birth,
A supernova beaconed in the East,
And the universe emerged into the light
Along with my perception of
The planet Earth.

Naked I came from my mother's womb…
The Lord giveth….Praise be the Lord. (1)

The night
Stretches in a milk-white haze across the sky
As distant as I can see,
As far as the stars extend.
Immersing my eyes in the ocean of light,
I stand like Ptolemy on the pivotal rock
With the lamps of heaven in orbit around me,
World without end.

You will never understand the world aright
Till the sea itself floweth in your veins,
Till you are clothed with the heavens
And crowned with the stars. (2)

Whatever exists…
Indeed, that anything exists that does exist
Is reason for wonder --
Unaffected, unalloyed.

What is more understandable,
What makes more sense,
Is not anything,
Nothing.
An entropic vacuum,
Darkness,
A void.

But, if I am to believe my senses

(And what else should I believe?)
I am at the centre of a heaven
With a saraband of stars.
In the morning
I see the sun rise in the East;
In the evening
I see the sun sink in the West;
In the night above me
I see the stars and planets
Pirouetting across the dark.
The universe revolves about me.
After I am dead
The dance will end --
Or so I like to imagine;
So I like to pretend.

"You are extraordinarily self-centred", she said.

"I am. I admit it.
But I cannot escape myself.
The six cubic feet or so I occupy
Wherever I stand
Travel with me
And will continue to do so
Until I am dying,
Until I die,
Until I am dead."

"As I was saying", she said,
"Extraordinarily self-centred.

But then, so am I."

Empty my glass, but still the bottle flows
And still the clusters ripen in the sun.
In brandy sleeps the wisdom of repose
While God keeps fretting what He might have done
And Linda sniffs the bosom of a rose.

Most wisdom lies in retrospect.(3)

Had I the opportunity,
Were I to start all over,
Back at the beginning, so to speak,
Before existence had begun,
Before the Big Bang,
Before Satan and sinning,
Before the birth of the sun --
To be specific:
Book of Genesis, Chapter one, Verse one --
I would handle it all quite differently,
Regard it, so to speak, as a Re-creation
Based on the experience
Of what I had previously done.

Ah, Love! could thou and I with Fate conspire
To grasp this sorry Scheme of Things entire,
Would we not shatter it to bits -- and then
Re-mould it nearer to our Heart's Desire? (4)

To start with,
I would generate at most a Little Bang,
And, given the necessary activation energy,

Create a smaller, non-expanding universe
No larger than the Solar system
And free of *sturm und drang;*
Measured not in light-years
But miles or light-seconds,
More manageable, easier to control,
Without all these extraneous galaxies,
Black holes and multitudinous stars
In flux and flow,
Red-shifting in chaos and worse,
Rendering the unwieldy even more…
Even more so.

Shifting majestically
From the insignificant to the sublime,
I would restore planet Earth
Once more to the centre of this universe.
I would dispense with the chancy mechanism of evolution,
Of Darwinian natural selection,
Of survival of the fittest,
So wasteful of species
And extending over such a tedious time.
Instead
I would revert to that more efficient hands-on procedure
Prescribed in the Scriptures
Whereby I (the Omniscient Author),
As the outcome of my intelligent design,
Would, in just six days,
Bring to birth
All the fauna, all the flora,
All the beasts of the field, all the birds of the air,
All the flowers of the forest,
That presently share our habitat Earth.
And since all power that is real exacts that it be visible
(As exemplified by the Messiah),
I would sit enthroned on the summit of Mount Olympus
In authority over My Creation.
This time around I might well omit
Several strains of bacteria,
The mosquito, the mamba, the arachnid, and the rat;
And from previous eras I might restore
The trilobite, tyrannosaurus rex, and other exotica
Such as the woolly mammoth and the australopithecan cat.

As matters presently stand,
On this planet Earth
A strutting biped dominates the land
Pouring concrete on the green,
Pumping poisons in the air,
Fishing to exhaustion the sea,
Fouling its habitation,
And leaving its five-toed footprint in the sand.

Let us pray to our Father
Let us pray to our Lord
That our planet abide by
The Kyoto accord.

Difficult to acknowledge,
Easier to forget
That this strutting biped,
This reigning monarch of the animal kingdom
Is itself an animal.
It does not care to think so, and yet ...
Is it not subject to the organic cycle
Of birth and life and death?
Does it not eat and excrete,
Reproduce,
Feel pain,
Draw breath?
If you prick it,
Does it not bleed?
If you tickle it,
Does it not laugh?
If you poison it,
Does it not die?
And if you wrong it... (5)
In short,
Just a hair-diminished mammal
Adrift on a cosmic ocean.

Every living being is also a fossil (6)

Nevertheless,

Acknowledge the creature
Is a sapient original,
Undeniably wondrous
Thanks to its convoluted cortex,
Its superior brain,
Capable of good and evil,
Of creativity and destruction,
Of the profound
And of the profane.

We are human and yet we so quickly forget
The species to which we belong.
In the midst of the slain we say never again
But belligerent instincts are strong.
For the stigma of Cain is humanity's stain
And the passion of Abel our song.

Our Father who art in Heaven
Pray let me live on Earth
In comfort and tranquility,
Prosperity and mirth.

Before me on the screen
I see skeletons of poverty
Struggling in overcrowded shanty towns
Crudely built like open-sore latrines;
I see the torments of hunger, of skin-tight bones
On the barren desert soil;

I see shattered dwellings and crumbling stones.
I see the scars of violence on the flesh of refugees,
Families stacked with bric-a-brac
Stumbling from persecution on buckled knees
Toward the camps where hope has been abandoned.

I sometimes wonder how many,
At any moment in time,
Couples are copulating?
Children are being conceived?
People are dying?

Broken bodies, bleeding minds,
Anguished vision of the dead;
As civilization's trappings fall aside
Reduced to the animal core,
A core of pain, of raw and ruptured thought
Which some exploit for gain and some for sport.

Do not, I entreat you Lord God
(Or whatever Fate, if any, governs my being),
Allow me to be exposed like this;
The veneer to be stripped away
So that I am revealed in all my nakedness,
Pitched into the maelstrom of survival where
To still the crave that gnaws my gut
I'd renounce my beliefs for a cup of water,
Or for a crust of bread my friend betray.

Once upon a time (or, to be more precise, on 18 April, 1906) there was a ranch on the outskirts of San Francisco owned by some folk called Shafter. Early in the morning, one of the Shafter's cows was standing near the barn, awaiting the arrival of dawn. At around 5 a.m., the ground began to tremble and the earth to fall apart. And when the quake had subsided, all that could be seen of the cow was the tip of her tail sticking above the ground. We should do well to remember the Shafter's cow, a hapless victim of immense forces about which she knew nothing and which, in less than a minute, reduced San Francisco to ruins and buried her in oblivion. (7)

As it is,
I have to accommodate my physical needs.
Even Achilles had to unbuckle his armour
And squat.
Even a Queen in her widows weeds

Liked to consort with her gamekeeper.
And I sweat when I am hot.

As I sit here on the loo,

Scatological thoughts coursing through my head,

Proctological visions encumbering my brain,

I imagine the battleship Tirpitz

Floating in the porcelain fjord below

In full view

Of myself, the bomb aimer,

In a Lancaster plane

Bent on destruction

In this circumscribed main.

Then…how shall I say?

Elimination!

Bombs away!

And a palpable hit egad.

Witness then

My mind at play

And the triumph of ordure!

Along with anaesthetics, the other unambiguous benefit of the twentieth centuryhas been the sewage system. But we are no more aware of this system than weare of the workings of our digestive tracts. No, it is cyber space or whateverthat commands our attention, not sewage disposal. (8)

So be it --

This winning biped struts the Earth

Cocooned in self-applause,

Ashamed of primal origins,

Transcending Nature's laws,

Prefers to couple in the dark

And shit behind closed doors.

Nevertheless,

Man is surely the closest likeness of God
That we shall ever encounter.
Meantime,
Money is the measure of all things:
We admire the rich; we pity the poor;.
But either way
And however much we may deplore
Man bears the indelible marks of his lowly origin. (9)

To be
We all need to eat,
We all need to excrete,
We all need to breathe,
We all need to sleep,
We all need to awaken.

And yes! To be!
That is the answer.
Not heroism or fame,
Not happiness or riches,
But survival.
To exist!
To be.

In terms of species, the objective fact of survival is more fundamental than the quality of the surviving life – good or bad. (10)

And yes, I really must remember to pay the Electricity bill.
It is long-time overdue.

In the garden of my childhood
The vision is gone but the fears remain:
Of the serpent slithering through the grass,
Of the brown-boned gypsy stealing me away.
Now, sat at my desk of polished rosewood grain,
I poise my pen above the empty page
Seeking the imagery for what I want to say,
Searching among the memories of old age.
Beyond the park, as it approaches the crossing
I hear the mournful cry of the evening train

Like the haunting loon in the shadows of the lake
Calls to the waters silvered by the moon.

"Thanks! I'll have a pint of beer.
Bitter for choice."

"Same here."

"Me too! And I agree –
The World Cup should be England's for the taking
Or just so long as Beckham's on the ball."

"There's some that say he's got a gammy knee."

"And others that he's heading for a fall."

"Who cares!"

"Me! I care.
Implore Almighty God that we should win.
And by a quite substantial score."

"And should -- so I suppose.
But does God care?"

"Not God! Nor I!
In my view all these contact sports
Simply an outlet for testosterone:
Concussion or a broken nose,
A fracture of whichever bone,

A swallowing of steroids."

"Yet as I've said often before --
A World Cup better far,
Far better than World War."

"Cheers! And as you say
Better by far than war."

"Take my word,
Be it prayers for victory
Or to mourn defeat's disgrace,
No more absurd
Than seeking God's support
For other contests in this human race."

"Amen!
And the meaning of life –
Do you wish to know?
I will tell you.
It is 'Go Leafs! Go!'"

In the nocturnal sky above the city
Eternity is rendered invisible
By the electric haze where bulbs abound.

"There's supposed to be
A fireworks display tonight."

In the nocturnal sky above the city
Silence is rendered inaudible
By the cacophony of urban sound.

"Fireworks to shatter the silence,
To fill the sky with coloured light."

*"Lighten our darkness, we beseech Thee O Lord,
And by Thy great mercy defend us from all perils and dangers of this night." (11)*

In the marble portico
Of the city bank
Below whose night-lit panes
Birds and angels lie shattered,
A panhandler beds on the stone
Pillowed by a plastic bag.

"The bottle in whose grasp I hide,
The void where joy and anguish meet,
Has dulled my brain and drowned my pride
And left me falling on my feet.

Along the corridors of time
Your voice I hear, your face I see,
And if you can't afford a dime
Then spare a little love for me."
The strings of hope are out of tune
And day is   almost done.
We must avoid or be destroyed
By whomsoever points the gun.
The melanomas of the moon,
The carcinomas of the sun.

"Any spare change, Mister?
Display your solicitude.
Bring comfort to my bed.
Any spare charity?
Thanks Mister!"

Bring out your dead!

We are all in the gutter, but some of us are looking at the stars .

Along the sidewalks, evening revellers,
Unaware of planetary motion,
Mindless of the cosmos above
And of the waste land below,
Respond to neon invitations,
To a seductive face,
To offers of oblivion in a bottle,
To twenty minutes of commercial love.

Christ came from a white plain to a purple city, and as He passed through the first street, He heard voices overhead and saw a young man lying drunk upon a window-sill. Why do you waste your soul in drunkenness? He said. Lord, I was a leper and You healed me; what else can I do? A little further through the town, He saw a young man following a harlot and said Why do you dissolve your soul in debauchery?, and the young man answered Lord, I was blind and You healed me; what else can I do? At last in the middle of the city He saw an old man crouching, weeping upon the ground, and when He asked why he wept, the old man answered Lord, I was dead and You raised me into life, what else can I do but weep? (13)

Where are you Athanasia Pallas?
Are you hiding in my dreams?

Since my baby left me
Found a brand-new place to dwell.
It's down at the end of Lonely Street
At Heartbreak Hotel. (14)

The jungle beat of rock and roll
Guitared and overstrung;
Lyrics compliments of the million monkeys
Chained to a collective keyboard,
While screaming teens in skin-tight jeans
Hysterically give tongue
To a culture of frivolity
That magnifies the young.

"With rock and roll plugged in your ear
And your mind awash with wine or beer,
How can you enjoy a conversation?
How can you think?
How can you even hear?"

"I enjoy swing and the crooning of Bing
And jazz sets my senses astir.
Country and rapping may start my toes tapping
But rock-and-roll rhythm is what I prefer."

"It's a cool time at the equator.
It's a hot time at the pole.
But whatever the heat
I embrace the beat
When they play that rock and roll.
Yes! When they play that rock and roll."

"Such music is the nectar of my soul,
This plug its conduit.
O O O O that Shakespearean rag --

It's so elegant
So intelligent. (15)
And all at the press of a button
On my digital cellular phone. "

"From his Republic
Plato banished the poet.
Then how much more compelling that we
Should silence these raucous youth,
These opium-swilling, needle-fixing,
Smoke-imbibing, booze-befuddled, dope-dead junkies,
Suppress their din,
Their jungle beat,
And as we cool their prickly heat,
Allow the voice of poetry in."

"But now this youthful cacophony….
It has become the voice of poetry."

"God forbid!"

At his elbow, a pint of bitter
Which he will drink,
Pour down his vacant throat,
Down, down the sink,
Down, down the drunken drain.
A chemical conversion of the brain
To inhibit thought or, perhaps, to help him think.

"Last orders, ladies and gentlemen!"

"My tankard, landlord!
Another pint if you please!
And pints for my friends."

Beer is proof that God loves us and wants us to be happy. (16)

"Time gentlemen please!"

"With so much time to kill,
What weaponry with which to kill it?"

"Boredom or liquor;
Maybe falling ill?"

"Then sicken and so die
Or what you will." (17)

"Perhaps abandon hope?"

"Pray pass the butcher's knife
Or hangman's rope
And let me think how I might end my life."

"Perish the thought!
There's too, too much to live for."

"Like what, old sport?
Like what?"

"Like lecherous encounters,
Bacchanalian banquets,
Whatever turns you on,
Your lust's delight.
There is a Feast of Fools.
This very night."

*"Let us go then you and I.
Let us go and make our visit.(18)*
But where? Where is it?"

"That whorehouse where the madame, Oyster Moll,
A dominatrix arrogant and cruel,
Enforces strict subservience,
With all her patrons subject to her rule."

"Her whips, so rumour says, are *sans pareil*,
And Oyster Moll herself notorious

As flagellant for whom it's fit to die."

"Perchance she'll whip some wisdom into us."

:"She'll try, I guess."

And yes I said yes I will yes. (19)

"Give me a hundred milligrams of meth-amphetamine, good apothecary, to accelerate my imagination." (20)

The wheel rotates on the axle of time
Scything through sleep
From which we dead awaken,
Another life.
Another dream forsaken.

Atoms that spin in lattices of light
And molecules invisible as air,
While galaxies and stars wheel through the night
Through space and time fused in the light-year,
Occupying dimensions that lie
Outside the purview of the seeing eye.

If a pile of dimes the height of the CN Tower
Were to represent the duration of the universe
From the beginning of space/time,
Then the existence of homo sapiens
Would be about the thickness of one dime.

Where the telescope ends
The microscope begins.
Which of the two
Has the profounder view? (21)

If each molecule in a raindrop were recognisably marked
And the drop evenly distributed
Throughout the oceans,
Then in every drop of sea water,

There'd be some dozen marked molecules

In my imagination's eye
New visions I create;
Cascades of colour, sculptured shapes,
And objects animate;
Evolve new forms, possess new worlds,
And life illuminate.

In my imagination's mind
New matter I design
By mixing disparate ideas
To see how they combine
Or changing oil to ethylene
Or water into wine.

But there are magnitudes my mind
Cannot conceive at all
And where imagination's gaze
Confronts an opaque wall
Like billions or a billionth,
The very large, the very small.

In between
The dimensions of the universe
And the dimensions of an electron
Lies Man -- the mean.

No! I am not J. Alfred Prufrock, nor was meant to be.
Here I am
Sat at my desk of polished rosewood grain,
I poise my pen above the empty page
Seeking the imagery for what I want to say,
Searching among the memories of old age.
Beyond the park, as it approaches the crossing
I hear the mournful cry of the evening train
Like the haunting loon in the shadows of the lake
Calls to the waters silvered by the moon.

"My sermon is taken once more
From the Book of Genesis, Chapter one, Verses one to ten -
In the beginning or even before,
God created the heaven and the earth....
World without end
Amen."

"In my belief
If there will be no end,
Then there was no beginning --
Like the circle.
Or if there was a beginning,
Then there will be an end --
Like the line.
Time, I believe, is irredeemable;
And everything that exists in time
Has always existed
And will always exist."

"All very well --
But what of the Creator?"

"Without a beginning
What need of a Creator?
There is not a time when I did not exist,
Nor you, nor all these kings. (22)
Superstitions of thousands of years
Are rendered irrelevant through the mysteries of physics --
Of relativity and quantum mechanics,
Of string theory and the structure of matter,

And of the principle of uncertainty.

"Uncertainty, yes.
But I comprehend. Blind as I am, I see.
Incidentally, what of the Big Bang?"

"A suspended moment
Between the blue shift and the red shift,
Between the red shift and the blue shift
In a pulsating universe
Where that which is
Is that which was
Is that which will be,
Explosion leading to implosion,
Implosion leading to explosion;
Galaxies created and disintegrated,
Disintegrated and created;
Extending the boundaries of space/time,
Contracting the boundaries of space/time;
The circle of space, the cycle of time,
Diastole, systole,
Positive, negative,
Plus, minus
Day, night,
In pulsations of approximately
Twenty billion years,
Governed by one absolute--
The velocity of light."

"Perhaps?
Or then again –
Perhaps not?"

"Definitely perhaps!
Or more probably, improbable.
Just fragments of wisdom

In a confusion of speculation
Most of which is beyond comprehension."

"I am alpha and omega,
The beginning and the end",
Saieth the Lord. (23)

"I am hubris and nemesis,
The creator and the destroyer",
Saieth the Lord.

Our bishop when he takes his tea
Likes to invite the Trinity
And so sits down to buttered toast
With Father, Son , and Holy Ghost;
While masticating noisily,
They analyse the Heavenly Host.
Benedictus. Benedicat.
.Hostia laudamus.

"I grow weary of the Father.
I grow weary of the Son.
And I grow aweary of the Holy Ghost.
But stating my opinion
Should you think I might have none,
It's God the Father wearies me the most."

In the trial of God the Father
(And of His two co-defendants
And of Zeus, Jehovah, Mohammed, Krishna, the Buddha,
And Whomsoever),
The Plaintiff, Homo Sapiens, charges that
He, God the Father, displayed criminal negligence
In his creation of the Plaintiff,
Namely the mammal Homo Sapiens.

Sitting in Judgment:

His Worship the Honourable Omniscient Author.

The Chief Prosecutor, aka the Plaintiff,
asserts that:
"Homo Sapiens splendent on its throne
Would seem to be enrobed in high estate,
But stripped to skin is merely flesh and bone
And physically a puny vertebrate,
Itself in conflict with itself within
That fragile skull where brute and angel reign,
Where virtue is cohabitant with sin,
This mammal's one distinctive mark -- its brain,
A brain that is aware that it must die
And knows some answers to the question What?
But when confronted by the question Why?
Is baffled by what is and what is not."

The Judge, aka His Worship the Omniscient Author,
addressing himself :
"When it comes to arbitration
The Judge shall ignore
The Chief Prosecutor's comment about the question Why? "

Chief Prosecutor:
"Why, Your Worship?"

The Judge:
"Because it is not in evidence.
Please to proceed."

Chief Prosecutor:
"Throughout history, Your Worship, people have believed in the innate goodness of Humanity and have assumed that, given the proper utopian

conditions, be they freedom from economic struggle or simple back-to-nature existence, communities could live together in happiness and brotherly love. Events of the last century must surely have convinced all but the blindest optimist that this is not so. It is fair to say that the great majority of Humanity are selfish, motivated by thoughts that are

seldom rational, are idle, lustful, and show no sign of moral advancement. This is in no sense a condemnation, simply a statement of fact. It would be as foolish to berate them for this as it would be to condemn them for having two legs, a heart, hair, or what you will."
(24)

In His rebuttal

The Defendant, aka God the Father, asserts that:

"God may do exactly as He pleases.

I am God.

Therefore I may do exactly as I please."

In his summation

The Judge, aka His Worship the Honourable Omniscient Author, states that:

"Whereas the Defendant's argument, with its distributed middle,

Is logically impeccable,

The premises on which the argument is based are false.

Therefore the verdict is: Guilty as charged.

And the sentence is: Atheism

Whereby everybody is forbidden to believe in the divinity

Of the Defendant, God the Father,

Including Himself."

Plaintiff:

"No doubt He will appeal. But to whom?"

The Judge:

"To whomsoever will listen,.

But I still haven't paid my Electricity bill."

That man is the product of causes which had no prevision of the end they were achieving; that his origin, his hopes and fears, his loves and his beliefs, are but the outcome of accidental collocations of atoms; that no fire, no heroism, no intensity of thought and feeling, can preserve an individual life beyond the grave; that all the labours of the ages, all the devotion, all the inspiration, all the noonday brightness of human genius, are destined to extinction in the vast death of the solar system, and that the whole temple of Man's achievement must inevitably be buried beneath the debris of a universe in ruins -- all these things, if not quite beyond dispute, are yet so nearly certain that no philosophy which rejects them can hope to stand. Only within the scaffolding of these truths, only on the firm foundation of unyielding despair, can the soul's habitations henceforth be safely built. (25)

My life has genial been throughout the years,
And apprehensively I contemplate
Approaching death. A soothing faith I need
To nullify the burden of my fears --
A loving God, eternal life hereafter,
The transmigration of my fictive soul.
Even the flames of hell a better creed,
More comforting than a vacuum,
More acceptable than oblivion.
But get thee behind me Satan!
To confront reality -- that is my goal.

"I do not believe in God the Father Almighty
Maker of heaven and earth
Or in Jesus Christ His only Son our Lord.
I do not believe in the Holy Ghost,
The holy Catholic Church,
The Communion of Saints,
The Forgiveness of sins,
The Resurrection of the body,
And the Life everlasting,
Amen." (26)

The tribes dividing humankind shall bleed
From wounds of ancient wrong or present greed,
Of social contract or religious creed.
The desperadoes in today's redress
Kill thousands with the triggers that they press
While spore-like in a silo sits a bomb
Able to dig this living planet's tomb.

*For every human being on Earth, there exists nuclear explosive
equivalent to three-quarters of a ton of tri-nitro toluene (TNT). (27)*

High on the rostrum the fanatic stands
Backed by emblems, festooned with flags,
Serenaded by voices, by military bands,
Immune to reason, blind to light,
And set in concrete that he's right,
Violence exploding from his tongue,
A diatribe 'gainst evils done the tribe,
Looking down like God
On the mindless adoration of the multitude below
Hypnotised as one in the worship of its leader
Believing Him divine.
Ten thousand throats
Squealing affirmation,
Transformed by the demon Circe into swine.

*God and country are an unbeatable team;
they break all records for oppression and bloodshed. (28)*

"Let our discontent be a stimulus for action,
And let us be guided by patriotism,
By the glory of the Motherland
Or the Fartherland or the Nearerland,
For then it were a privilege
To die --
In a blaze of crimson
Like the setting sun
Or even obscurely
In the filth of the gutter

Eviscerated, bleeding
For the glory of Whateverland."

Breathes there a man with soul so dead
Who never to himself hath said
"This is my own, my native land" (29)

"Ten thousand throats
Squealing affirmation,
United against a common foe:
Whoever,
Whoever's different,
Anyone different will serve the purpose,
Black or White,
Gentile or Jew."

"Might is right!
Anyone different will do."

Those who can make you believe absurdities
Can make you commit atrocities. (30)

In the Tower of Babel
There were many inhabitants.
And the Lord said, Behold
The people is one, and they all have one language.
Let us go down and there confound their language
That they may not understand one another's speech.
So the Lord scattered them abroad from thence
Upon the face of all the earth. (31)

But language is a gulf that actions may bridge,
Whereas divides more lethal, wider divides,

Fester in tribalism with its long-ago wounds
Or in the worship of a different god
Or even disputes over the same god
Or pigment of the skin or slant of eye
Or universal schism --
That between
The impoverished many
And the wealthy few.
Might is right!
Rich and poor!
Vae Victis!
Resolution -- War!

When the banner is unfurled
All reason lies in the trumpet.(32)

"Let us promote peace and eschew violence.
Let us highjack their aircraft and smash them into their towers.
Let us die for the cause and mount to Paradise,
Each with seventy-two virgins
To wile away the heavenly hours
With a cuddle and a kiss.
This we do truly believe;
And what a trivial price is the sacrifice
Of this little life
For a Martyr's eternal bliss."

"Whatever happens we have got
The maxim gun and they have not." (33)

"But what of all this talk promoting peace?"

"Judge people not by what they say but by what they do,
Not by their words but by their actions…
Besides these are just terrorists"

"Terrorists or Soldiers of God? It's a question of perspective."

Whatever crushes individuality is despotism
By whatever name it may be called (34)

Here endeth the Lesson.

In conformity's grey agreement

There is no internal dissent,

No conflict among those who conform.

In this Utopia

Each is clothed in the same dress

Adopts the same cliches

Is bound by the same norms

Thinks the same thoughts

Abides by the same laws

Battles for the same cause

And marginalizes those who differ.

In democratic society, flattery takes the form of saying to people they are like other people rather than possessing something peculiarly their own. (35)

If all humanity conformed to the same image,

Worshipped the same god,

And shared the wealth equally,

There would be no war.

Here resumeth the Lesson.

"In my youth

How humiliated I felt

To be wearing threads out of fashion.

I imagined the contemptuous stares

And side-of-the-mouth criticisms.

So uncool! So uncouth!"

The part in each of us that is individual

Has special value
And is the part each of us tries to suppress. (36)

"So much of my life spent wanting --
Wanting the approbation of my peers,
Wanting to be envied, popular,
To be charismatic and strong.
But most compelling of all:
Wanting to belong."

"Where is my John the Baptist
To prepare the way for me?
To lead me out of the wilderness?"

"Where is my Salome
To demand the Baptist's head upon a charger?"

"Let us set out in search of the Holy Grail."

"On behalf of the species
Let the search be for Peace."

"On behalf of the individual.
Let the search be for Happiness."

"But alas! We are doomed to fail."

By contrast
In diversity there is adversity,
Contrary perspectives provoking antagonism
And generating original thought.
In a Utopia of absolute agreement
We might still be protozoa
Floating in the ocean's embrace
And multiplying by dividing.
Meantime, as I see it,
The only prospect for uniting humankind
Is an invasion of aliens from outer space
Or infection from some virulent pandemic
Which, taking advantage of inter-continental air travel,

Might unite our species
With the threat of our extinction.

If anything be done to a system in dynamic equilibrium that would result in a change in any of the factors determining that equilibrium, the system will adjust itself in such a way as to minimize that change. (37)

"We will crush dissent in our pursuit of liberty.

We will sanitise our nation by ensuring the purity of our people.

We will manufacture weapons of defence so that we can mount attacks.

We will wage war in the interest of peace.

Whatever needs to be done

We shall do it,

With either a bomb or a gun."

Lechery, lechery, wars and lechery,
Nothing else holds fashion. (38)

"I believe", said Bill, "that it's wrong to kill.

I reckon it's for peace that we should strive."

"Can't agree", said Fred, as he shot him dead.

"Myself I'm very glad to be alive."

At Passchendaele

The terrain is pockmarked with craters,

And flesh -- theirs and ours--

Drowns in the sludge.

But in retrospect

The battlefield assumes a romantic aura

With bodies buried in a blaze of beauty.

In Flanders fields the poppies blow
Between the crosses, row on row,... (39)

"For the Fallen
In transport to heaven,
Let us now sing Hymns Ancient and Modern
Number twenty-seven:
Abide with me, fast falls the eventide.
The darkness deepens; Lord with me abide.
When other helpers fail and comforts flee,
Help of the helpless, O abide with me. (40)"

"Myself,
I liked the raw excitement of it all --
Life honed to a fine awareness,
Feeling the pulse of the passing hours,
While threatened by
The omnipresent thrill of death.
I liked the simplicity:
All problems and responsibilities set aside
And living focused on a single purpose – victory.
Onward like a never-turning tide;
Onward to victory."

Roll out the barrel;
Let's have a barrel of fun.
Roll out the barrel;
We've got the blues on the run. (41)

"I liked the fellowship, the cameraderie,
The letting-down of social barriers,
And the intercourse of voices who had never conversed before.
Myself, I enjoyed the war."

But
At a time of crisis,
Or whenever a tyrant disposes,
Civil liberties may be suspended.

First they came for the Jews
And I did not speak out
Because I was not a Jew.

Then they came for the Communists
And I did not speak out
Because I was not a Communist.

Then they came for the trade unionists
And I did not speak out
Because I was not a trade unionist.

Then they came for me
And there was no-one left
To speak out for me. (42)

At four o'clock in the morning
There is a savage hammering at the front door.
"Political Police! Gestapo!"
Whether to confront them or to hide?
To run or to reside?

Leather-coated, trilby-hatted,
Grey-suited. jackbooted.
More fearful is the terror that comes by night
Than the arrow that flies by day.

In the confrontation between Good and Evil,
Fought on the battlefield of the mind,
God may champion Good
But the advantage lies with the Devil.
God is so tedious
Whereas the Devil may revel
In Evil unconfined.

Villie Boger, vilest soul,
Hung his victims from a pole.
Bludgeoned them to make them swing.
Bludgeoned flesh to make it sing.

"But even my speech-machine cannot persuade the dead to talk",
admitted Boger

It is easier to destroy than to create
And, as incentive to fight,
There is nothing more powerful than hate.

Hate is an antidote to fear. (43)

Give me a gram of prozac, good apothecary,
to bring a little pleasure to my torment. (44)

I have within me
The goodness of my brother John
And the evil of Reinhard Heydrich.
So, I assume, does everybody.
I am Cain, I am Abel.
So, I assume, is everybody.
There is nothing good or bad
Of which I am incapable.
So, I assume, is everybody,
Even my brother John.

Obscure and terrifying little acts
Accomplished in loneliness and deep security
Mark out our limitations more surely
Than great crimes. (45)

I live in a balanced environment
With killing confined to inanimate objects
Like smashing a seven iron
That has failed to plant my Topflight on the green;
Indeed has drowned it in the pond.

Said the little fishes with a grin
"Why what a temper you are in." (46)

I have yet to experience
The full horror of human depravity,

And except in my imagination,
I don't suppose I ever will.
At Auschwitz,
The epitome of all that is vile in the human experience...
At Auschwitz,
The Anus Mundi of the inhuman universe...
At Auschwitz where,
In moments of masochistic tension,
My imagination has sometimes sought to incarcerate me...
Auschwitz was defecated by the Devil
Into a cesspit of evil.

All nations, it seems, are guilty of atrocities,

But some appear guiltier than others --

A viewpoint that may be influenced by

The nation to which one owes allegiance.

At Auschwitz, for Sunday sport, the S.S. Scharfuhrer called over a couple of Jews, ordered them to dig a grave, and told them to lie in it. They obeyed. The Scharfuhrer then ordered a Polish prisoner

to bury the Jews alive. "I had rather not, Herr Scharfuhrer", replied the Pole. The Scharfuhrer hustled the two Jews out of the grave and ordered the Pole to lie down in their place. He then ordered the Jews to bury the Pole. Terrified, they began shovelling earth on top of him. But before the Pole had been completely covered, the Scharfuhrer ordered him to climb out and the Jews to get back in, re-establishing the original scenario. This time the Polish prisoner responded to the Scharfuhrer's order with alacrity and buried alive the two Jews. (47)

Herded beside the railroad tracks
Meandering into the unknown afar,
Rifles prodding at our backs,
They pack us in each cattle car.
The multi-coffined transport grinds
Across the miles of space and time.
Women scream, children cry.
Our huddled bodies and our minds
Wallow in excremental slime.

People are happy in different ways
But in sorrow they are as one. (48)

A crack in the boards reveals
Whether it be night or day,
But not, alas, where we are going.
"To a work camp" they had said.
But without food and water
Ere we arrive
Many of us will be dead.

Eventually,
A slowing down, a halting lurch,
The doors flung open,
And stark outside our stinking cell
A cankered copse of bush and birch,
And vision of the gates of hell.

On Birkenhau's ramp
Backed by the stark silhouette of the arrival shed,
We who have survived the journey
Detrain into the horror of the night;
A night of black,
Of howling dogs,
Of shouting guards,
Of probing searchlights,
Of Strauss waltzes,
Of terror's attack.

Cruelty has a human heart. (49)

We parade before the Angel of Death
For the purpose of selection,
Whatever his whim may recommend,
Wherever his white-gloved baton points,
Some to the left, others to the right,
Standing apart,
Unaware of the different outcomes --
Execution or slavery,
The gas chamber or the camp,
Immediate death
Or a protracted end
In which,
Without time to adapt,:
Our being is obliterated,
Our selves are destroyed,
While we strive to survive,
Those of us who determine to survive,

In a hell of
Relentless terror
Death and panic
Starvation
Excrement
Scattered corpses
Rats and lice.
Beyond Satanic imagination –
Himmler's paradise.

When I was a boy
I had a cyanide bottle.
Butterflies that I trapped inside
Flapped their iridescent wings in desperation,
And died.

The road to heaven
(An S.S.joke)
Leads through the changing room
Where the 'merchandise' –
The old and infirm,
The mothers and their children,
Those directed to the left --
Divest their clothing;
And the guards
Seeking to calm them,
Seeking to deceive,
Hand to each
A peel of soap,
Herding them into the air-tight chamber,
Forcing them in with boot and shove,
Then slamming shut the door.
In mindless hope
They watch the sprinkler heads above,
But from each head pour out the fumes of death.
They scream and scratch, they clutch and claw,
The stifling poison on their breath.
The guards peer through the Judas hole,
And soon there is no sight, no sound,
No vestige of a living soul

As bodies yield to cyanide,
Batch-processed on the killing ground
Of bureaucratic genocide.

According to Adolf Eichmann:
"The death of a hundred is a tragedy.
The death of millions is a statistic."

The death of one, an Ann Frank say,
Is a tragedy with whom we can identify.

After they locked him in the gas chamber
And the crystals of Zyklon B were discharged through the roof-trap,
Did Doctor Pangloss still assert
"Everything is for the best
In this best of all possible worlds."? (50)
Or did he give way to despair?
Did he curse heaven and renounce God?
Who knows? All that remains is silence.

Lo sleep is good, better is death,
In sooth, the best of all were never to be born. (51)

Entwined the tortured corpses lie.
They must be untangled
And the gold fillings extracted.
Thence to the crematoria and up the chimney
Where salvation is signaled
By the odour of burning flesh
And by flame and smoke.

At Auschwitz
You arrive by the door
And depart through the chimney.
Another S.S. joke!

"There is some Ischariot in the Eternal Now ," said the Victim, "who might have saved me. But alas, he is dead."

And from each stack, thick clouds of black
Above the chimneys swirled,.
Said the Victim: *"What may be cannot be." (52)*.

And horror whispered at my back
"Oh what a lovely world."

Be happy, you who live in fine apartments, in ugly houses or in hovels. Be happy, you who have your loved ones, you also who sit alone and dream and can weep. Be happy, you who torture yourselves over metaphysical problems, and ...you the sick who are being cared for and you who care for them; and be happy, oh how happy, you who die a death as normal as life, in a hospital bed or in your homes..(53)

Ultimately,

Most people are unconcerned about genocide,

Just as long as it is others who are being slaughtered,

Just as long as it is another race which is dying or has died.

Indeed, there is some satisfaction in another's suffering

In comparison with which one's own may seem diminished.

I cried because I had no shoes until I saw the man who had no feet. (54)

"Fuck you, Jack! I'm all right!"

Life everywhere is life, life is in ourselves and not in the external....This idea has entered into my flesh and blood. Yes, it's true! That head which created lived by the highest life of art, which acknowledged and had to come to know the highest demands of the spirit, that head has been cut from my shoulders.... But my heart is left me, and the same flesh and blood which likewise can love and suffer and desire and remember; and this is, after all, life. On voit le soleil! (55)

"But damn it! I still haven't paid my Electricity bill."

To President Franklin.D Roosevelt, 2 August 1939.

Sir ...(succinctly stated)

It might become possible

To set up a nuclear reaction

In a large mass of uranium

Whereby a vast quantity of power

And of radioactive elements

Would be generated....

(Consequently, we believe that)

A powerful bomb could be created
(Which) carried by a boat
And exploded in a port
Might well level the port to the ground
Together with some territory around.
Yours very truly, Albert Einstein

"Line up the opposition against the wall,
The traitors and the cowards,
Enemies of the people.
Lock them in the Tower.
Massacre them. Shoot them.
Every one of them all.
Do not spare their naked lives."

Six Imperial swine,
Five wandering Jews,
Four Fascist dogs,
Three American tycoons,
Two Communist spies,
And a jailer with a jail key.

Incidentally,
In the end-of-war Dresden raid,
Nellie the hippo,
Detainee of the Dresden zoo,
Survived the firestorm.

"In time of war
There is no right or wrong,
No voice of dissent.
No compassion,
Only force.
To fight to the death is all that matters -
Without pity! Without remorse!
Death is the ultimate heroism."

Here dead we lie because we did not choose
To live and shame the land from which we sprung.
Life, to be sure, is nothing much to lose
But young men think it is, and we were young. (56)

"What is more
It is we, the victors, we who won the war,
Who decide what is moral,
Who establish the rules,
Who lay down the law."

"Some say the world will end in fire,

Some in ice,

Some with a bang,

And some with a whimper.

I don't know.

What do you say?"

Technological progress is like an axe in the hands of a pathological criminal (57)

To make an atomic bomb

Take two hemispheres of plutonium or enriched uranium

Each weighing some fifteen kilograms.

Take care to keep the two hemispheres apart.

At the moment of truth

Bring the two hemispheres together to form a critical mass,

Add a few neutrons and stir.

Stand back to observe the ensuing chain reaction

In which there is fission of the atomic nuclei ,

Loss of mass,

A massive release of heat energy,

And the transmutation of the original element

Into radioactive strontium and xenon and whatever...

All flesh is as grass.(58)

At 2.45 a.m. on Monday, August 6, 1945,

Colonel Paul Tibbets Junior and his crew

Took off from Tinian Island

In a B 29 called,

After the pilot's mother,

Enola Gay,
And travelling at a speed of 320K/hr
Arrived over the city of Hiroshima
At 8.15 a.m. Japanese time,
And taking as aiming point
The Aioi bridge,
Dropped a uranium bomb called Little Boy
Weighing some four-and-a-half tons
On the city.

Again:
What may be cannot be. (59)

Forty-three seconds later
At 1860 feet
The bomb exploded
Outdazzling the sun,
Blackening the day,
Flattening the buildings,
Paving the streets with radiation,
Ascending into a mushroom cloud
(Without a silver lining),
And killing a hundred thousand people or more.

Bring back the fathers!
Bring back the mothers!
Bring back the old people!
Bring back the children!
Bring back the human being
I had contact with.
For as long as there are human beings
Bring peace, unbroken peace.(60)

Three days later
Plutonium Fat Man was dropped on Nagasaki.
So ended
Another war to end all wars.

Now I am become Death,
Destroyer of worlds. (61)

But What if the Nip or the Hun
Had come up with the bomb before?
(Hirohito and Hitler rejoice!)
I would have been a radioactive child,
A victim of the war,
And deaf as the dead to every grey voice.

"Yet how should Man with his superior brain
Inflict such misery on his human kind?
How should he suffer such pain?"

*If our species is to survive,
We shall need a substantially new manner of thinking. (62)*

"No intelligence!
Intelligence is a bore;
*'tis not so sweet now
As it was before. (63)*
It's fouling up the planet;
And will kill us what is more."

*"Killing is the name of the game.
Those who do not accept that
have to be prepared to accept the alternative -
Defeat. (64)*
Besides, I was simply obeying orders."

"You enjoy free will.
You could have exercised choice."

"Free will is an illusion.
The choice was predetermined.
We are all of us puppets
With our strings in the hands of the Omniscient Author.
I tell you --
No-one is responsible for what they do.
As for myself,

I was simply one man obeying orders.
And if it hadn't been me...."

"Which is how the war began --
With the giving of orders by one man."

The existence of the hydrogen bomb presents a perfectly clear alternative to all the governments of the world. Will they submit to an international authority or shall the human race die out? (65)

Beware the orator

Charismatic of voice

Who can seduce reason,

Charm the emotions,

Play upon prejudice,

Who can orchestrate a crowd of many

Into a rabble of one.

Beware of such an orator;

For he may be a Shiva of destruction

Rending peace into pieces.

As he triggers the gun.

"I keep telling you:

I was simply obeying orders."

If there must be trouble, let it be in my day that my child may have peace. (66)

No! I am not T.S. Eliot, nor was meant to be.

But here I sit

Seeking the imagery for what I want to say,

Searching among the memories of old age.

Beyond the park, as it approaches the crossing,

I hear the mournful cry of the evening train

Like the haunting loon in the shadows of the lake

Calls to the waters silvered by the moon.

Einstein never grew weary
Searching for a unified theory
That would contain
The macroscopic and the microscopic.
But he searched in vain.
Just after one a.m. on April 18, 1955
Albert Einstein died in Princeton Hospital
From a burst aortic aneurysm
And probably in some pain..
mc squared = E.
R.I.P.

As for unity,
The Schrodinger wave equation
Embraces most of physics and all of chemistry. (67)
But as yet
There is still no Unified Field Theory.

Humanity's triumph:
The scientific imagination
Interpreting the nature of the universe
In equations and laws,
In metaphors,
In the mathematics of probability,
In effect and cause,
Subject to modification
As dictated by experience
And by the probing of new technologies,
Technologies themselves the product of science,
Which, alarmingly,
Is nowadays increasingly funded (and hence controlled)
By bureaucrats, generals, and business tycoons,
Leading to applications which have transformed the planet Earth
And afforded us, for better or worse,
Greater dominion over our habitat,
Bringing us to the age of information from the age of stone
And beyond -- into the unknown.

Any sufficiently advanced technology is indistinguishable from magic. (68)

On April 12, 1961,
The Russian cosmonaut Yuri Gagarin

Rocketed into space in Vostok 1,
Orbited the Earth,
And returned to terra firma.

If you feel like me, I guess you've found
You get sort of bored walking on the ground;
There's hills to climb and the cement's too darned hard.
But they tell me about this Gagarin guy
And it gets me itching to explore the sky
So I build a rocket in my back yard.

When I get to looking about the place,
Guess it seems sort of empty up here in space --
Just those no-good sputniks circling round and round.
I feel sort of cramped with my knees all bent
And my back all creaked and my weight all went.
So I reckon it's time I thought about getting down.

I get burnt up back in atmosphere
'Cause my chute won't open and my wheel won't steer;
And I land at sea and I swim way back to shore.
So now I'm home in my own back yard
And though I'm finding that cement hard
I won't go climbing up the sky no more.
No sir!

Through the Hubble telescope
Looking back in space,
Back through several billion years
May we hope to trace
In the forming galaxies
God Almighty's face.

As God created Man in His own image
So Man created God in his.

If triangles could think,
God would be eminently triangular. (69)

When Man first observed God,
He thought what he saw was good.

But alas, the act of observation
Changes that which is observed --
Relatively speaking
But uncertainly understood.

God, it seems, has been belittled by science.
"Indeed, Your Imperial Majesty, *God is become an unnecessary hypothesis."* (70)

We, the Gods of the universe,
These doubters shall dispel.
We must restore the mystery in our religions,
The spiritual dimension,
Along with the promise of Paradise, of sexual orgies,
And in order to fill our empty temples,
The threat of Hell.

"I Vishnova
Am the one true God.
All praise to Allah,
Allah be praised.
Jesus is My prophet,
The Buddha is My son.
Those who believe in Me
Shall enjoy death everlasting
Oblivious to pestilence and sorrow
With no today and no tomorrow.
Those who reject Me
I sentence to a life beyond the grave,
Of sleepless nights and tedious days,
Consumed by pain in Hell's eternal blaze."

"My God is clean shaven."

"How weird! My God has a beard."

"To represent God as bearded is piliferous."

"To represent God as clean-shaven is profane."

"Who will rid me of these intolerable priests?" (71

Black king's knight to White king's bishop - check!

White king's knight to Black king's queen - checkmate.

"Our conflicts to identify the one true God,
To demonstrate that my God is bigger than your God,
Have led to the slaughter of millions.

"Arguably God is insane."

"The peace of God that passeth all understanding,
The Father, the Son, and the Holy Ghost
Be with you and remain with you always."(72)

"I do not care whether God is;

And if God is,

Then who God is.

But this I assert:

If God is,

Then life is a tragedy --

That so much suffering exists.

If God is not

(And as I gaze into the heavens

It seems to me we are alone),

Then life is a comedy

And we must suffer the pain of life on our own."

Let us weigh the gain and the loss in wagering that God is. Let us consider the possibilities. If you gain, you gain all. If you lose, you lose nothing. (73)

You can make your life a misery if you try.

You can take a smile and change it to a sigh.

But why not throw off that shroud

And then look beyond the cloud

'Cause there's an awful lot of sunshine in the sky.

"Nevertheless, the infidel must be eliminated,

Expunged from the surface of the Earth."

"But we have eliminated the infidel so often before."

"Say what you will,
It remains a reason for war."

"Reason!
What reason?"

"Who cares!"

"But there has to be some underlying purpose."

"Does there? Why?
Anyway, purpose is retrospective.
Purpose is whatever happens to happen."

According to my veterinarian, she (my female Lhasa Apso) is experiencing a false pregnancy and believes the rubber ice-cream cone (which I gave her) to be a puppy. She hides it in closets. She carries it up and down the stairs. She is even secreting milk for it. She is getting shots to make her stop doing that. I observe how profoundly serious Nature has made her about a rubber ice-cream cone -- brown rubber cone, pink rubber ice-cream. I have to wonder what equally ridiculous commitments to bits of trash I myself have made. Not that it matters at all. We are all here for no purpose, unless we can invent one. Of that I am sure. The human condition in an exploding universe would not have been altered one iota if, rather than live as I have, I had done nothing but carry a rubber ice-cream cone from closet to closet for sixty years. (74)

"Who cares!
Who cares if there's a purpose.
Who cares if there's a reason
As long as we have guns,
As long as killing's open season."

Another reminder! If I don't pay soon, the Electric Company 'll be cutting off the power.

Thirty pieces of silver
Was the price of the Saviour's life.
They opted for crucifixion
But they could have used a knife.

On the Saviour's second coming
Over us all to reign,
Once more he went unrecognised
And was crucified again.

Eloi, Eloi, lama sabachthani. (75)

Let the Saviour come a third time
But trailing clouds of glory
With choirs of angels singing
And it might be a different story.

In this world of material possessions,
Of stately homes and drinking water,
Of precious stones and chocolate cake,
Mein Gott.
There are those who have
And there are those who have not.

God asked a man of the Sudanese Dinka tribe "Which shall I give you black man? There is the Cow and there is the thing called What?. Which of the two would you like to have?"

The man said "I do not want What?."

Then God said "But What? is better than the Cow."

The man shook his head. "No", he said.

God said "If you like the Cow, you'd better taste its milk before you choose it."

The man squeezed some milk into his hand and tasted it. "Let us have the Cow", he said. "And let us never see What?."

Later, God gave What? to other peoples, and it became the source of their acquisitiveness and scientific invention. (76)

There are those who have everything

And want more.

There are those who have nothing

And want everything.

Give or take,

This is another reason for war."

There is no beauty in the finest cloth if it brings squalor and unhappiness. (77)

Some diet on veggies and fibre;

Some diet on platters of meat.

But the diet of those who are starving

Is not having enough to eat.

"In this world ambitious for power,

Power of body, power of mind,

With ultimate authority

In power over life and death,

Power becomes an aphrodisiac craving for more,

Leading to persecution and paranoia

And to the elimination of all opposition.

This is another reason for war."

A country should be considered the more civilized the more the wisdom and efficiency of its laws hinder a poor man from becoming too poor or a powerful man from becoming too powerful. (78)

The hand that holds the gun is master.

The gun itself represents power.

Children armed with AK 47s

Wander the streets in an orgy of killing.
Their strength resides in the bullet.
Murder is easy. Death is cheap.
Bodies are burning in the fields.
The cemeteries are overflowing,.
The women weep.

"Who killed Cock Robin?"
"I", said the Sparrow,
"With my bow and arrow,
I killed Cock Robin." (79)
For all except the sadist,
Easier to drop a bomb from thirty-thousand feet
Or to fire a gun at a mile-away target
Than to kill another human face-to-face.
Easier still
To wring a chicken's neck
Or raze a plague of vermin without trace,
But not so easy
To kill another human face-to-face.

Then again, easy enough
To enumerate a human out of his identity,
To disgust a human out of his dignity,
To caricature a human into a less-than-human face,
To starve a human into apathy,
To torture a human out of all humanity,
To transform a human into an object of revulsion,
Into a musselman, an automaton, awaiting Death's approach.
Then it is easy enough

To lift a boot
And crush it like a roach.

"Why?", I asked Stangl (Commandant of the death camps Sobibor and Treblinka), "if you were going to kill them anyway,
What was the point of all the humiliation? Why the cruelty?"

"To condition those who had to carry out the policies." he said.
"To make it possible for them to do what they did." (80)

And thanks,
I'll have another slice of strawberry shortcake;
And tomorrow the German tanks
Will cross the Polish Corridor
As yesterday the Myrmidons
Discharged their arrows into the Trojan ranks.

I cannot but conclude the bulk of your natives to be the most pernicious race of little odious vermin that nature ever suffered to crawl upon the surface of the Earth. (81)

"According to Clausius …
According to the Second Law of Thermodynamics,
The energy/mass of the universe
Is constant; whereas
The entropy of the universe
Is tending towards a maximum.
In this enforcement ,
Resulting in descent from order to chaos,
The Second Law is a curse."

Respond to life with love.
Respond to love with joy.
Know what is appropriate
And adjust your reactions to the part
As if you are pretending to be human.
Open your eyes to the beauty.
Open your ears to the melody.
And *do not walk through the fields in gloves. (82)*

"According to Murphy's Law:
If there is anything that can go wrong,
It will.
In particular,
There is a conspiracy of the Public Transport Commission
Always to have me, whatever time I go to the stop,
Just to miss the bus."

"Then again,
Is there no voice…
Is there nothing to be said

About domesticity and marriage,
About children and family,
The foundations of existence,
Sometimes content,
Sometimes even happy?"

"A toast to the living"

"And a toast to the dead."

"Cheers."

People's finest works bear the persistent marks of pain. What would there be in a story of happiness? Only what prepares it, only what destroys it can be told. (83)

They say I have a tumour in the turmoil of my head
With maybe just a month or two to live,
But ere I cross the river to the kingdom of the dead,
I've words to write and people to forgive.

Before my questing eyes is spread the star-bright universe,
The mysteries that space and time reveal;
And driving down the thoroughfare of heaven in a hearse
Is God the Father sitting at the wheel.

There is no purpose to discern; there seems no reason why?
Only the wonder that it is at all.
And empty words are blown like smoke across an empty sky,
And wisdom's blind before an opaque wall.

So I sit here snorting caffeine in the parlour of my soul
And like the tide my feelings ebb and flow.
It seems I am a prisoner who has been denied parole,
And God knows what's the answer. Does He know?

Give me a fix of heroin (or coke or crystal meth or mandragora, even a bottle of Scotch), good apothecary, to sweeten my life perspective. (84)

We carry within us the wonders we seek about us.
There is all Africa and her prodigies in us. (85)
Or if anything is not within,
Then it's sure to be posted on the Internet,
That altar ego of the information age
Whose God is Pythagoras,
Whose Son is Babbage,
Whose Holy Ghost is Bill Gates,
Whose Virgin Mother is Ada Lovelace,
Whose Word is the Binomial Theorem
Whose Devil is the Virus,
And whose Bible is the Website.

With the world wide web at our fingertips
We may know at the press of a key
The mating habits of the African elephant
Or the timetable of every bus in Tokyo;
What Cicero said two thousand years ago
Or what President Bush said today.
And as the mountain of knowledge grows
Exponentially, year by year,
So avalanches of information
Cascade down the side
Burying wisdom beneath the slide.

Triple w Love dot com
Is where I get my jollies from.
No commitment and no regret

With intercoarse on the internet.

What I do when I get the itch,
Is sit me down, press the power-on switch;
Start off down that cyber trail
That leads me to some sweet femail.

Then when I get to feel keybored
I can switch her off without a word.
Rid myself of my computer spouse
With just the clicking of a mouse.
So there's megabliss in megabites
And googling adds to its delights.
Not a connection you'll forget
Intercoarse on the internet.

From the Big Bang to the Abacus,
From the Abacus to the Mac,
We have advanced into a robotic world
Where we have lost our mental grip
And become dependent
On the intelligence of the silicon chip.

Where is the Life we have lost in living?
Where is the wisdom we have lost in knowledge?
Where is the knowledge we have lost in information?
The cycles of Heaven in twenty centuries
Bring us further from God and nearer to the dust. (86)

"How widely have I travelled? Since I was a boy

I have experienced many times and many places.
I fought with Hector at the gates of Troy.
Jesus I witnessed scorned by accusing faces.
I stood among the riff-raff at the Globe
Applauding Shakespeare at his actor's trade.
I saw King Charles divest his royal robe
And bow his head before the axeman's blade."

And like a dying lady lean and pale
That totters forth wrapped in a gauzy veil
The moon arose up in the murky East
A white and shapeless mass. (87)

On Sunday 20 July, 1969,
The Eagle landed
At the edge of the Moon's Sea of Tranquility
This side of heaven.

Armstrong followed by Aldrin
Stepped on the lunar surface,
Armstrong saying:
"Just a small step for Man (or a man).
A giant step for Mankind."
They remained for twenty-two hours; then
Returned to Apollo 11.

Aman, Amen.

"Here I sit
Before the television screen
As if it were a mirror
Reflecting my emptiness,
A stage that the actors have vacated,
A page from which the print has been erased.
Just a few fabrications
Ambiguously stated
Of what might have been;
A few experiences
Preserved in the formaldehyde of memory,
And, of course, the occasional interference
But otherwise empty and extending
From parturition to paradise
With a little life between.

"'Why not escape?' you say.
But where?
There is nowhere else to go."

"Here I sit
Before the television screen,
Sit where I sat yesterday,
And the day before,
The days, the days before,
Mind captivated
In the straitjacket of indolence,
Paddling on the remote

From channel to channel
(Give us this day our daily bread)
Opening or closing this or that door."

"See 'Desperate Housewives' last night?
Riot they were."

"No! I was watching Cold Case Files.
Murder and rape.
Real life for the viewer's delight."

"It's my experience
The life we live on the box
Is so much more engaging;
And yes, I am grateful to television
For allowing me to live by proxy."

"Sure!
Don't know how I'd survive
Without another world in which to escape."

Into a culture of computers and cellular phones,
Of Harry Potter, Mama Mia, and the Rolling Stones.

I've got a strange addiction
For adolescent fiction.
Folk think that's cool
But believe it's hotter.
Right now the thing I need
Is a thrilling book to read
Like Harry, Harry, Harry fucking Potter.

Outside my window
A maple spreads its branches

Perilously over a rooftop,
But the lakes and woodlands of my childhood,
Harmonious and green,
Have been supplanted by electronic circuitry
Tracing the world on a glass screen.
In this suburban sprawl
I am distanced even from my own species,
Connecting with others hardly at all.

"There is always somebody in the other room
And you don't quite remember who it is
And you are surprised when they make a sound
Or go down the hall to the bathroom..
But there isn't always somebody in the other
room because sometimes there isn't another room
and if there isn't sometimes there isn't anybody here at
all." (88)

On the phone
I listen to recorded voices;
On the computer
I network with faceless minds;
At the bank
I negotiate with a machine;
And before the television
I blank out in a substitute world,
Living vicariously in whatever the remote may program,
Living by proxy through the actors on the screen,
Living what might have been,
A life of luxury, a broken heart;
Circuitry designed to bring us closer
But dehumanizing
And keeping us further apart.

In the room the women come and go
Talking of Michelangelo. (89)

"Mummy, what shall I do?"
But I am too old for mummy to help me.

Besides, mummy's dead.
Instead
I must respond on my own to my boredom
If that may be done;
For if I drink oblivion of a day
So shorten I the stature of my soul.(90)
Boredom -- the ultimate enemy
Against whom the battle is never won. "

Au contraire
We cannot stop the birds of sorrow flying overhead
But we can prevent them from nesting in our hair. (91)

With the exception of humans
Other subjects of the animal kingdom
Demand little more of life than to live =
To eat and to excrete,
To copulate and to sleep,
To breathe and to be,
To survive and to die.
They do not require that life have meaning;
They do not ask why.

In the illusion of choice
I look back on what might have been
And it compares favourably with what was.
It seems I have experienced it all before.
I regard the past with regret
And the future with anxiety.
Sure! Life is a bore!

And in today's youth culture,
They no longer heed the wisdom of the old.

"Sufficient unto the day is the tedium thereof."

"Henceforth I shall look to life to imitate art."

The genius of humankind –
Imagination's throne -
Composing symphonies from sound,
And making shapes from paint and stone,
And through the poetry of words
To render feelings known.
Whatever's beautiful it seems
A sense of soul affords --
The Mona Lisa's haunting smile
And Bach's majestic chords,
The marbles of Praxiteles,
And Shakespeare's silver words.

Humanity's triumph:
The artistic imagination
Revealing the beauty and wisdom of the universe,
Of organic life on this planet,
Of the human condition;
With shapes of metal and stone
With patterns and layers of colour
With words of verse and prose
With cinematic versatility
With symphonies of sound,
The artist, as if the Almighty's clone,
Explores the range of human emotions;
And out of whatever he or she may find
Creates imaginative truth,
Comprehensive and profound,
And establishes connections between matter and mind.

Great artists are those who dare to confer the right of beauty on things so natural that people say on seeing them: "Why did I never realise before that that was beautiful too?" (92)

"A critical question is
Does the animal homo sapiens have a soul?
If yes, do other animals have souls?
Plants come to that?
And where anatomically is the soul located --
In the magician's hat? In the pineal gland?"

"So be it!
For Godly faith,
Belief in a hereafter,

No preacher more persuasive speaks
Than Death,
Our species cursed
In our foreknowledge
That life be terminal,
With sermons of the void,
Terrors of nothingness,
So at the moment of our dying breath
We call on God, whoever God may be,
'Lord God of Hosts
Wilt Thou abide with me?' "

"So be it!
But immortality,
That salve for which we pray,
That deliverance which we crave
To carry us beyond the pain of flesh,
Beyond the dusty darkness of the grave,
Is just a fanciful illusion.
Better to seek the soul in DNA."

Let's praise the double helix,
Let's honour DNA,
Because it has been programmed
To shape our living clay.
But then let us appreciate
And then let us beware
That DNA's indifferent:
The helix doesn't care.

"So be it!
But what of living? What is life?"

"Life is the animation of the inanimate
Within the framework of a cell.
Life lives imprisoned in a cell."

"Then what is death?"

"Death is the termination of life,
Of release from the cell,
Of the restoration of the inanimate,

Of the Second Law,
Of the status quo."

"What d'you know!
Always incarceration =
The cell or the grave."

Here endeth the lesson.

Organic shapes on this terrestial stage
Transfigured by that ancient Gorgan Time
To stone,
Petrified,
Fossils from another age
Those many million years ago alive;
Precursors of the future
In shapes that still survive.
The origins of *homo sapiens*
Coffined in the rocks;
Australopithecan bones buried in the sand;
Cave paintings,
Monolithic carvings,
Pieces of pottery
(Epoxy make thee whole!),
And fragments of antiquity --
Hieroglyphs,
The Pharoah's tomb,
The peasant's bowl.

Through the lexicon of the rocks –
Pages of Earth history –
The past speaks
In layers of grey voices.

It is as an astronomer or a geologist that I have a real perspective on life, humanity, and the universe. (93)

"As I grow old, grow deaf, grow blind,
It is not so much
That I lose touch with reality

As I lose interest.
For I have known them all already, known them all-
Have known the evenings, mornings, afternoons.
I have measured out my life with coffee spoons. (94)
And the prospect of a day without tomorrow
Is no longer unappealing."

So when the world looks sombre,.
You've given up all hope,
And it's clear that every prospect's gone awry,
Time's come up with your number.
Grab a gun or find a rope
For the moment has arrived for you to die.

Let's look on the suiside of life.
Let's, let's look on the suiside of life;
'cause wouldn't it be grand
To expire by your own hand.
Let's look on the suiside of life.

Looking down from this building,
Looking down like a Peeping Tom,
Down at the midgets meandering on the street below,
I am momentarily seduced
By what I know is an irreversible moment
(Like the press of the doomsday button)
Alluring me, hypnotising me,
Into plunging from the rail --
A fatal aphrodisiac;
And as I fall,
Fall in a wave of ecstasy,
Will there be an instant of regret
As I am falling, fall,
Accelerating at a rate of
32 feet per sec/ per sec
Give or take…?
And yet not yet I say.

Instead, I step well back.
I shall not terminate today.

Fear of death
Spawns so much concern
About the existence of a soul,
About a congenial life hereafter,
About song and laughter,
After that last breath.

Sat at my desk of polished rosewood grain
I poise my pen above the empty page
Seeking the imagery for what I want to say,
Searching among the memories of old age.
Beyond the park, as it approaches the crossing,
I hear the mournful cry of the evening train
Like the haunting loon in the shadows of the lake
Calls to the waters silvered by the moon.

All thoughts, all passions, all delights,
Whatever stirs this mortal frame;
All are but ministers of Love,
And feed his sacred flame. (95)

Of Love there is a myriad of manifestations:
Of parent for child,
Of child for parent,
Of friend for friend,
Of lover for lover
Of self for self
World without end....

Remember who kept telling you he loved you only
And guaranteed that none should lead his heart astray.
But now you're gone, and from now on when I feel lonely,
I often dream a little dream of yesterday.

"I love you."

"I love you too."

Sustain me with raisins; refresh me with apples, for I am sick with love. (96)

True love is an illusion,
As the cynical explain.
Its fulfilment comes to nothing,
Its promises are vain,
Its pleasures soon degenerate
To platitudes and pain.
It's a fever that enflames the mind;
And yet withal I am resigned;
Although this love be no more lasting
Than snowdrops in the spring
I'll take whatever love may bring.

Love's the enchanter,
Makes rainbows in our eyes.
Love is understanding
Past the wisdom of the wise.
Love is that unseeing wing
On which we humans rise.
It is the cynics I despise.

In the union of love I have seen,
In a mystic miniature,
The prefiguring vision of the heavens
That saints and poets have imagined. (97)

Love may be worship or lust,
Joy or torment.
It may be joyous torment
Or tormented joy.
It may be all of these at once,

May ennoble or destroy.

Love may degenerate
From passion to indifference,
From trust to jealousy.

Whoever loves entertains jealousy involuntarily. Some there are who do not sleep; for in the wide-awake corridors of their brains , there pads a restless demon who has crawled out of the darkness –

woken from the sleep that eludes them. (98)

In the unity of Love
The child may be conceived.
In the appetite of Lust
The child may be conceived.

Testosterone driven,
My thoughts and actions determined
By that ridiculous up-and-down appendage
Dangling between my legs.

Give me a tablet of Viagra, good apothecary, to achieve a resurrection. (99)

In the name of Love
Great crimes have been committed,
Great deeds have been accomplished,
And heads have been laid upon the block.

In the courts of Love
There is no redress.
The tide flows in
And the tide flows out
And the waves lap at the foot of the rock

For love, my love, there is no room
Within our litany.
The protean shapes our loves assume
Breed ambiguity.
Our dancing eyes, our paddling hands,
Our clasping in a kiss
Are but the urgings of our glands,

And love we should dismiss.
Yet one last time indulge me pray
Before my senses yield.
I love you. Never more I say.
Henceforth my lips be sealed;
And though I worship you all else above,
Ah no, I shall no longer love you, love.

Beware of paradoxes in love.
It is simplicity which saves,
Simplicity which brings happiness. (100)

At my boys' boarding school
I was taught Latin;
I was taught Divinity.
I discovered how to masturbate.
But I never found out which female buttons to press
Or even that there were buttons.
I came to believe that, for women,
Sex was a sacrifice that
In order to conceive,
They were willing to endure,
Resigned to the discomfort
They were obliged to face.
I learned about love from black-and-white movies
In the back row of the cinema
While furtively sneaking a tentative embrace.
I am now wiser,
But I remain unable
To integrate lust and love,
And copulation I find aesthetically so unattractive
That I would now rather worship the goddess
As in my blushing youth.
Then again,
Sometimes I lie to myself
In the belief that I am telling myself the truth.

Truth is the domain of philosophers. In human relations, lies are more important. Humanity can stand only a little truth. (101)

No, it is not the birds of sorrow flying overhead.
It is Ibsen's wild duck nesting in my skull
That makes life supportable.

I publish the banns of marriage

(Or of union, partnership, one-night stand, or whatever)

Between XY Bachelor of the parish of Epsom

And XX Spinster of this parish

Anticipating they will live together in a state of matrimony

(Which may or may not be holy)

Until distance or divorce do separate them

Or death does them part.

"And yes, my dear,

And yes, I am alone.

I'm sorry but

You should be old enough by now to know

That love is for the young,

And if I sometimes seem engulfed

By the sea of long ago,

Nevertheless the vision is gone,

The illusion is no longer supportable,

The flesh of desire is turned to stone;

And the old bull dreams in the shadow of the tree

Ignored by the rest of the herd.

So was our loss,

And I was Judas at my own betrayal,

But it was she who laid me on the cross

And it was she who hammered in each nail.

The flesh of Love her malice crucified,

And it was Love upon the cross that died.

In the interlude between the beginning and the end

This couple may or may not generate children,
Establish a family,
Dwell in a domestic habitat that is governed by
Joy or anguish,
Security or incarceration,
Stimulation or boredom.
Either or both may suffer a so-called broken heart.
Or live happily ever after.

This alone is certain:

She who once was the helmetmaker's beautiful wife ((102)

Has been shrivelled by the sculptor into a living cadaver;

And Rita Hayworth, my teenage goddess,

Died of Alzheimer's.

Sooner or later in life, everyone discovers that perfect happiness is unattainable, but there are few who pause to consider the antithesis: that perfect unhappiness is equally unattainable. The obstacles preventing the realization of both these extreme states are of the same nature: they derive from the human condition which is opposed to everything infinite. Our insufficient knowledge of the future opposes it: and this is called, in the one instance, hope, and in the other, uncertainty of the following day. The certainty of death opposes it: for it places a limit not only on every joy but also on every grief. (103)

Meantime Rita Hayworth survives in my memory,

Still dances in my aging brain,

Untouched by time,

Immune to pain.

In a fanciful world

Of astrology, fortune-telling, and UFOs,

Of alchemists, quacks, and the philosopher's stone,

Of naturopaths and psychopaths,

Of angels, conspiracy theories, and a benevolent god,

And of other *such stuff as dreams are made on (104)*

(Bearing in mind before I dismiss everything

That *there are more things in heaven and earth, Horatio*

Than are dreamt of in your philosophy).... (105)

In such a fanciful world

Illusion offers a spectrum of colourful possibilities --

Heaven and Earth forgive! --

Whereas reality is tedious and mundane
And irreconcilable with the way we wish to live.

The illusion that exalts us is dearer than a thousand truths. (106)

En passant
I was born under the sign of Libra
With the Sun in the Second House,
Mars in trine aspect to the Moon
And Saturn in the ascendant.
Consequently , I have nothing immediate to fear.
I may look forward to
A new romantic attachment
And a million-dollar lottery prize
Within the coming year.
Very pleasing. Very nice. Very unlikely.

Almost all prayer is asking God
To make two plus two equal five. (107)

In turn, divine providence is the tumble of the dice.

The universe of chaos
Is governed by its own laws.
In other words
Chance is deterministic.
Though whether chance is the cause
Or the effect
Who knows!

The Race is not to the swift nor the battle to the strong
but time and chance happen to them all. (108)

Humanity's triumph:
The artistic and scientific imaginations,

The mathematics of music, the poetry of mathematics;
The artistic vision and the scientific vision
Together discovering order in the chaos of experience
And demonstrating
The connectedness of all things.

A human being is a part of a whole called by us "universe", a part limited in time and space. He experiences himself, his thoughts and feelings, as something separated from the rest... a kind of optical delusion of his consciousness. This delusion is a kind of prison for us,

restricting us to our personal desires and to affection for a few persons nearest to us. Our task must be to free ourselves from this prison by widening our circle of compassion to embrace all living creatures and the whole of nature in its beauty. (109)

I am an old man at the fringes of the unknown

Toothless, incontinent - yes, *a paltry thing (110)*

Oscillating between a cadaver and a buffoon,

And still fearful of punishment,

Of the prefect's cane, of the adult's rebuke.

Here I lie

Stretched out on the bed,

Letting the nonsense on the screen

Trickle into my head,

Weary to be living,

Fearful to be dead.

Having clowned my way through life,

I now face my end in disbelief.

No special wisdom born of age I bring;

None I believe exists.

And I --

Not even an object of compassion

Unlike the wheel-chaired child

Broken, retarded

Mouth open, gazing at the sky.

Unlike the girl in terminal despair

Whose *cancer hath no pity on*

Blue eyes and golden hair. (111)

The Electric Company's final reminder! I begin to think I too, like my goddess, may be contracting Alzheimer's.

For us, the aged,
We try to feel gratitude to have experienced living.
We are concerned about our cholesterol count
And try not to complain that we must wither and die.
I have experienced the Creation.
I have dwelt in Paradise.
I have seen the Serpent and eaten of the Apple.
Now it is my time to endure the Fall.
For the scream of life,
The primal shout,
Must needs be obliterated by the silence of death.
Let me therefore respond in the spirit of Shandeeism:
The urge to carry on with a grimace or a shrug
Even after we've found life out. (112)

Along the corridor
Leading from the geriatric's room
Sterile and green,
Leading to the exit or the lead-lined womb,
Either an open door
Or through the morgue towards the uncharted shore,
Whichever this old body should dictate
Or gods decree
Or vagaries of fate.

And I looked,
And behold a pale horse:
And his name that sat upon him was Death,
And Hell followed with him.
And power was given unto them,

Over the fourth part of the Earth,
To kill with sword and with hunger
And with death,
And with the beasts of the earth. (113)

The surgeon gowned in antiseptic green
But now too late for chemo or the knife.
The ravages of toxic nicotine
Have stained the fragile nucleus of life,
Malignancy in every pore
Metastasised to every part;
And who is knocking at the door
In rhythm with my beating heart?

...it's better to die violently and not too old. People talk about the horrors of war, but what weapon has been used that even approaches in cruelty some of the common diseases. Natural death almost by definition means something slow, smelly, and painful. (114)

Along the corridors of my brain
Pads a restless demon,
A hag that seeks to render me insane
And against whom I must contend.
She is the nightmare that savages my dreams,
The succubus that transports me
Into the asylum of sleep
Where bodies burn in fields,
Eyes weep,
And I lie awake
As the cry of the loon on her nest
Haunts the fog-shrouded lake.

Love makes us poets, and the approach of death should make us philosophers. (115)

Give me a morphine cocktail, good apothecary, with which

To ease my suffering. (116)

For we are born in other's pain
And perish in our own. (117)

And now instead,
With no title, no possessions,
Behind which to hide,
I lie upon my hospitable bed
Absolved of all responsibility
For creating, relating, even for thinking…
Whatever they decide.

There is a time for many words and there is a time for rest. (118)

No duties to fulfill,
No promises to keep,
Simply to survive:
To eat and to excrete,
To breathe and to sleep,
Suffer the needles, swallow the pills,
Whatever they decide will heal the wounds
Or cure the ills.
But when the sole purpose of living
Is to stay alive,
Life becomes meaningless,
Reduced to that last breath
As I am left to encounter
The ungentle spectre of Death.

I do not fear death. I had been dead for billions and billions of years before I was born, and had not suffered the slightest inconvenience from it. (119)

If time were reversible,
If the womb would open up to receive me

And I were to dwindle to nothing
Terminating in an earth-shaking orgasm :
That were the apotheosis of my being.
How I would wish to die!
Wooden womb, ceramic urn:
Bring out your dead!
Body rot! Body burn!
Often I hear the creak of death
Within my aging bones.
Nurse! Nurse! Fetch a gurny.
I'm off on a long and a lonely journey.

So be it!
Entropy triumphs in the end.

As he lay dying on his bed
He whispered words to me:
"My ultimate concern", he said,
"Is where I put my back-door key?
And who will win the Stanley Cup?"
Whereon he slammed his eyelids shut
And left the world for dead.

Death is nothing to us, since when we are, death has not come;
and when death has come, we are not. (120)

No muffled drums, no slow march.
No tum tum ti tum Chopin funeral dirge.
No gun carriage, no burial in the Abbey.

For this corruptible must put on incorruption,
And this mortal must put on immortality.
For when this corruptible shall have put on incorruption
And this mortal shall have put on immortality;
Then shall be brought to pass the saying that is written:
Death is swallowed up in victory.
O Grave where is thy victory?
O Death where is thy sting? (121)

"Do you then want a conventional burial service?"

"Yes! But not for the belief.

I want it for the poetry."

In the grieveyard of voices.
There is only silence.
The fool babbles to himself
But nobody listens.
The man of religion preaches to himself
But nobody hears.
Ashes to ashes.
Dust to dust.
Will ye nae come back again?

Most people go the grave with their music still in them, (122)
Together with memorabilia that no-one else will remember
Like the hat-trick I bowled in a school cricket match.

In the cavernous sunset
Of my fading intellect
I still search for insight,
Groping in the falling darkness
And saying to myself
Only connect. (123)

By amalgamating disparate experience
Man may create something new,
Sometimes trivial, sometimes profound,
Make something
Where before
There had been nothing.
In Man's creativity
Lies his genius.
In Man's creativity
Is his greatness to be found.
In Man's creativity
His being is crown'd

Whoever is devoid of the capacity to wonder, whoever
remains unmoved, whoever cannot contemplate or know
the deep shudder of the soul in enchantment, might
just as well be dead for he has already closed his
eyes upon life. (124)

I am placed in a casket
And taken to a funeral parlour,
Or call it a funeral home,
Whichever sounds more comforting,
Set back in some suburban street,
A single-storied rectangular slab of bricks
Inside of which the walls are tastefully decorated
In pastel green and white.

The air is perfumed with polish and antiseptic,
And the staff are studiously polite.
The casket is carried to the Reception Lounge
Or some such euphemistic space
Where I am laid on an oak table
And the lid of the casket is removed,
Exposing
My cosmetized face
To the gaze of the curious --
Viewing I think they call it?
Just a preliminary social gathering
Where relatives and friends
Sip coffee and nibble egg sandwiches
("Give us this day our daily bread")
And reminisce about, criticize, even shed a few tears for
The dear departed, the troublesome dead,
And albeit broken-hearted
Are secure in the knowledge that they are alive,
At least temporarily;
Indeed, in the presence of death,
More alive than usual:
For it is the living who need to acknowledged,
Not the dead.
The dead don't give a flying ….!

Next mourning,
The lid is fixed back on again
Extinguishing the light,
Shutting out the world,
Blackening into a darkness

That the blind eye is unable to penetrate.
I am then removed to the funeral home chapel
Tastefully decorated in pastel pink and white
Where I am laid, sanitized and respectable,
Together with a smiling photograph,
On a table-clothed altar.

Ritual burial is the oldest form of collective symbolic activity. (125)

A hired non-denominational minister
Conducts the proceedings --
"Celebrating the life of ",,",", as they now call it,
Rather than bemoaning the death --
And in deference to my unbelief
He eschews any reference to Father, Son, or Holy Ghost,
Seeking to compensate for lack of spiritual sentiment
With profound secular allusions
And a hearty delivery
Designed to diminish grief.

My long-time friend then delivers a eulogy,
Entertaining the sombrely-suited acquaintance of the dear departed
With our long-ago escapades.
No music, no poetry,
Nothing to awaken the brain in the box.
Empty without ceremony,
And in need of ceremony
Even though the ceremony be empty.

The mourners --
Rather fewer than I would have anticipated --
File out in order of precedence,
Relatives first,
Sign a book of condolence
Reverentially indicating their attendance,
And retire for lunch to the Reception Lounge
Where they are released from sorrow into a jocund humour,
Distancing themselves from death
With the fanciful belief

That my newly-released spirit
Floats companionably among them
Reassuring them of my life hereafter
And vicariously enjoying the cucumber sandwiches.
"He always did like cucumber."

However,
Not in fact requiring lunch,
My mortal remains are carried by pall-bearers
To the cremation parlour
Where this incombustible shall put on combustion
And this inflammable shall be consumed in the flame.

I am removed from the coffin
(or was it a casket?
Whichever, why waste it?),
Slid into the gas-fired cremator
And, after eighty minutes calcination,
Reduced to molecules of carbon dioxide and water
Together with a residue of some five pounds of ash
Which, in accordance with Thermodynamics' Second Law,
Neither God nor all the king's men
Can put back together again.

We brought nothing into the world
And it is certain we take nothing away.
The residue of ash is gathered in an urn
And bequeathed to my eldest son
Who will scatter it to the winds.

And some there be that have no memorial
Except an alabaster helix that I carved,
A few verses that I wrote,
And four contributions of DNA.

And yes, as always,

Entropy triumphs in the end.

On the horizon

The restless sea,

Unmindful of human aspirations,

Indifferent to the poet's pen,

Broods over our destiny.

Responsive to the moon,

The tide flows in,

The tide flows out,

And the waves lap at the foot of the rock.

In this grey fog

There are many voices,

Most of them mine.

Fragments of thought,

Fragments of sound,

A confusion of elements.

In life's periodic table.

"Who will disperse the fog?"

"Only the Critic may do that."

"Sir indeed, the pruning knife!"

"Zounds man, the axe!" (126)

"Where is my Ezra Pound?"

What have I learnt?
On the one hand:
On every flower, there is a butterfly.

On the other hand:

There is a scorpion under every stone (127).

And so

The Electricity has been cut off,

Never to be restored,

And *the lamps are going out all over Europe. (128)*

The only certainty

Of which I am absolutely certain

Is my eighty-year life-span

Together with all my experiences therein.

"Naked I came out of my mother's womb

And naked I shall return thither.

The Lord gave, and the Lord hath taken away.

Praise be the Lord." (129)

Searching among the memories of old age,

Seeking the images for what I want to say,

I poise my pen above the empty page,

Sat at my desk of polished rosewood grain…

And now

As my own grey voice

Becomes inaudible,

The rest is turbulence.

World without beginning,

Amen.

Life is a loon…alone.

REFERENCE NOTES:

1. *Book of Job 1:21*
2.. Thomas Traherne
3.. Hoblyn
4.. Edward FitzGerald -- *Rubaiyat of Omar Khayyam*
5.. William Shakespeare - *Merchant of Venice*
6. Jaques Monod
7. *The Dynamics of Change* (Kaiser Aluminum, 1966)
8. Hoblyn
9 Charles Darwin
10 C.G.Darwin
11. *Book of Common Prayer*
12 . Oscar Wilde -- *Lady Windermere's Fan..*
13 Oscar Wilde
14. Tommy Durden.
15. T.S.Eliot -- *The Waste Land*
16. Benjamin Franklin
17 William Shakespeare -- *Twelfth Night*
18 .T.S.Eliot - *Prufrock*
19. James Joyce - *Ulysses*
20. William Shakespeare -- *King Lear*
21. Victor Hugo
22. Bhagavad-Gita
23. *The Revelation 1:8*
24. Primo Levi
25. Bertrand Russell
26. *Book of Common Prayer*
27 Hoblyn.
28. Voltaire -- *Candide*

29. Sir Walter Scott
30. Voltaire
31. *Book of Genesis 11:5*
32. Ukrainian Proverb
33. Hilaire Belloc
34. John Stuart Mill -- *On Liberty*
35. Wyndham Lewis -- *The Apes of God*
36. Andre Gide -- *The Immoralist*
37. Le Chatelier's Principle
38. William Shakespeare -- *Winter's Tale*
39. John McCrae -- In Flanders Fields
40. Rev Francis Lyte
41. Lew Brown
42. Pastor Niemoller
43. Not Known
44. William Shakespeare - (see note 12a)
45. Francois Mauriac
46. Lewis Carroll - *Through the Looking-Glass*
47. Anthony Hecht – from a poem *More Light! More Light!*
48. Primo Levi
49. William Blake
50. Voltaire –*Candide*
51. Heinrich Heine
52. Christian Morgenstern
53. Micheline Maurel - *An Ordinary Camp*
54. Russian proverb
55. Dostoevsky
56. A.E.Houseman
57. Albert Einstein
58. *1 Peter 1;24*

59. Christian Morgenstern.

60. Sankich Toge – Hiroshima Victim

61. Robert Oppenheimer- from the *Bhagavad-Gita*

62. Albert Einstein

63 William Shakespeare – *Twelfth Night*

64. William Donovan – Prayer for success of the Hiroshima raid

65. Albert Einstein

66. Thomas Paine

67. Paul Dirac

68. Arthur C, Clarke

69. Spinoza

70. Pierre Laplace

71. King Henry the Second

72 *Book of Common Prayer*

73. Blaise Pascal

74. Kurt Vonnegut - *Jailbird*

75. *St. Mark's Gospel*

76. Francis Deng -Dinka Myth from *Learning in Context*

77. Mahatma Gandi

78. Primo Levi - *If This Is a Man*

79. Nursery Rhyme

80. Gitta Sereny's Interviews with Franz Stangl

81 Jonathan Swift – *Gulliver's Voyage to Brobdingnag*

82. Frances Cornford – *To a Fat Lady Seen from a Train*

83 Andre Gide – *The Immoralist*

84. William Shakespeare – *King Lear*

85. Sir Thomas Browne – *Religio Medici*

86. T.S.Eliot – *Choruses from the Rock*

87 .P.B.Shelley *The Moon*

88 Charles Bukowski – *the other room*

89. T.S.Eliot - *Prufrock*

90 George Meredith – *Modern Love*

91 Chinese Proverb

92 Andre Gide

93. Bertrand Russell

94. T.S.Eliot - *Prufrock*

95. S.T.Coleridge

96 *Song of Solomon*

97. Bertrand Russell

98. Charles Baudelaire

99 William Shakespeare – *King Lear*

100 Charles Baudelaire

101.Graham Greene

102 Rodin sculpture

103 Primo Levi - *If This is a Man*

104 William Shakespeare - *The Tempest*

105 William Shakespeare - *Hamlet*

106 Alexandr Pushkin

107 Ivan Turgenev

108 *Ecclesiastes 9:11*

109 Albert Einstein

110 W.B.Yeats - *Sailing to Byzantium*

111 Not known

112 John Cowper Powys's Introduction to Sterne's *Tristram Shandy*

113 *The Revelation 6:8*

114 George Orwell.- *How the Poor Die*

115 George Santayana

116 William. Shakespeare – *King Lear*

117 Francis Thompson

118 Homer

119 Mark Twain
120 Epicurus
121. *1 Corinthians 15:54/55*
122 Disraeli
123. E.M.Forster -- *Howards End*
124. Albert Einstein
125 Terrence Des Pres — *The Survivor*
126. R.B.Sheridan - *The Critic*
127 Greek Proverb
128. Viscount Grey of Fallodon
129 *Book of Job 1:21*

The previous poem *is both good and original. Unfortunately the parts that are original aren't good, and the parts that are good aren't original. (Dr. Samuel Johnson)*

I should like to thank Allan Revich for arranging and handling the publication of this poem.

Hugh Oliver
123 Scadding Avenue - #863
TORONTO M5A 4J3

A CD of *A Fog of Grey Voiees* (recorded by the author and Athanasia Pallas) is available through www.hugholiver.com